# UNDERSTANDING
## The Bible

**The Message To Trust**

By the same author

BASIC CHRISTIANITY

YOUR CONFIRMATION

CONFESS YOUR SINS

THE EPISTLES OF JOHN: A COMMENTARY

THE CANTICLES AND SELECTED PSALMS

MEN MADE NEW

OUR GUILTY SILENCE

ONLY ONE WAY

ONE PEOPLE

CHRIST THE CONTROVERSIALIST

GUARD THE GOSPEL

BALANCED CHRISTIANITY

CHRISTIAN MISSION IN THE MODERN WORLD

BAPTISM AND FULLNESS

THE LAUSANNE COVENANT

CHRISTIAN COUNTER-CULTURE

UNDERSTANDING THE BIBLE     *Available in library
or paperback editions*


OTHER BOOKS IN THIS SERIES

THE PURPOSE AND THE PLACE

THE STORY OF THE OLD TESTAMENT

THE STORY OF THE NEW TESTAMENT

THE BIBLE FOR TODAY

# UNDERSTANDING
## The Bible

---

## The Message To Trust

---

## by   John R.W. Stott

*Understanding the Bible*

## SCRIPTURE UNION
**47 Marylebone Lane
London WIM 6AX**

**Published in the United States by
Regal Books Division, G/L Publications
Glendale, California 91209   U.S.A.**

© Copyright John Stott 1978
First published in *Understanding The Bible* 1972
Reprinted 1972, 1973,
Revised 1976
First published in this form 1978


ISBN 0 85421 619 7


U.S. Library of Congress Catalog Card No. 501 7602
ISBN 0 8307 0660 7

*Illustrations by Annie Valloton*

Printed in Great Britain by
McCorquodale (Newton) Ltd., Newton-le-Willows

# PUBLISHER'S PREFACE

UNDERSTANDING THE BIBLE has appeared in several editions, not only in the United Kingdom, North America, Australia and India, but in such languages as German, Swedish, Dutch, Spanish, Faroese, Japanese, Chinese and Thai. The author's objectives set out in his preface are being steadily fulfilled.

Now we are issuing the original publication in five separate volumes in a further attempt to achieve those aims. We anticipate meeting an even wider need; making readily available to new readers the individual subjects on which the Rev. John R. W. Stott has written so clearly.

Their use will not be confined to the individual reader; it will be practicable to use them in study and house groups, etc.

Each book contains recommendations for further reading and an index of scripture references referred to in the text.

# PREFACE

Every author owes it to the reading public to explain himself. Why has he thought fit to swell the torrent of books—especially religious books—which pours from the world's printing presses every day? Can he justify his rash enterprise? Let me at least tell you frankly the kind of people I have had in mind while writing. They fall into two categories.

First, the new Christian. With the spread of secularism in our day, an increasing number of people are being added to Christ and His Church who have no religious background whatever. Here, for example, is a young man from a non-Christian family. The Christian instruction he received at school was minimal, and possibly misleading. In any case the fashion was to pay no attention to it. He did not go to Sunday School as a kid, and he has seldom if ever been to church. But now he has found Christ, or rather been found by Him. He is told he must read the Bible daily if he is to grow into spiritual maturity. The Bible is a closed book to him, however—an unexplored, uncharted territory. Who wrote it, he asks, and when, where and why? What is its message? What is the foundation for its claim to be a 'holy' or special book, the book of God? And how is it to be read and interpreted? These are proper questions to ask, and some answer must be given to them before the new Christian can derive maximum benefit from his Bible reading.

Then, secondly, there is the Christian of several years' standing. In the main, he has been a conscientious Bible reader. He has read his portion faithfully every day. But somehow it has become a stale habit. The years have passed, and he himself has changed and matured as a person. Yet he has not developed as a Christian in any comparable way. A sign (and cause) of this is that he still reads the Bible as he did when he was a child, or a new convert. Now he is tired of his superficiality, his immaturity, and not a little ashamed. He longs to become an adult, integrated Christian, who knows and pleases God, fulfils himself in serving others and can commend the gospel in meaningful terms to a lost, bewildered generation.

My desire is to assure such a Christian that the secrets of Christian maturity are ready to be found in Scripture by all who seek them. There is a breadth to God's Word which few of us ever encompass, a depth which we seldom plumb.

In particular, our Christianity is mean because our Christ is mean. We impoverish ourselves by our low and paltry views of Him. Some speak of Him today as if He were a kind of syringe to be carried about in our pocket, so that when we are feeling depressed we can give ourselves a fix and take a trip into fantasy. But Christ cannot be used or manipulated like that. The contemporary Church seems to have little understanding of the greatness of Jesus Christ as lord of creation and lord of the Church, before whom our place is on our faces in the dust. Nor do we seem to see His victory as the New Testament portrays it, with all things under His feet, so that if we are joined to Christ, all things are under our feet as well.

It seems to me that our greatest need today is an enlarged vision of Jesus Christ. We need to see Him as the One in whom alone the fulness of God dwells and in whom alone we can come to fulness of life.[1]

There is only one way to gain clear, true, fresh, lofty views of Christ, and that is through the Bible. The Bible is the prism by which the light of Jesus Christ is broken into its many and beautiful colours. The Bible is the portrait of Jesus Christ. We need to gaze upon Him with such intensity of desire that (by the gracious work of the Holy Spirit) He comes alive to us, meets with us, and fills us with Himself.

In order to apprehend Jesus Christ in His fulness, it is essential to understand the setting within which God offers Him to us. God gave Christ to the world in a specific geographical, historical and theological context. More simply, He sent Him to a particular place (Palestine), at a particular time (the climax of centuries of Jewish history) and within a particular framework of truth (progressively revealed and permanently recorded in the Bible). So the following chapters are concerned with the geography, history, theology, authority and interpretation of the Bible. Their object is to present the setting within which God once revealed and now offers Christ, so that we may the better grasp for ourselves and share with others the glorious fulness of Jesus Christ Himself.

## NOTE

1  See Col. 1.19; 2.9, 10

## THE MESSAGE TO TRUST

Since the Bible is a whole library of books, composed by many human authors over more than a thousand years, it seems to some quite incredible that we can claim for it a single theme, let alone condense it into a single chapter. Besides, they say, do not the Old and New Testaments contradict each other? Does not the Old Testament portray Jehovah as a fearful God of wrath and judgment, who is entirely incompatible with the God and Father of our Lord Jesus Christ? How can we reconcile the thunders of Sinai with the meekness and gentleness of Christ?

I hope that the true answer to these questions will become plain as in this book I try to demonstrate further the astonishing unity of the Bible. Meanwhile, it will be enough to express the Bible's own claim that it contains neither a ragbag of miscellaneous contradictions, nor a gradual evolution of human ideas about God, as men grew up and discarded their childish notions, but a progressive revelation of truth by God.

1

Progression there undoubtedly is. For example, the great stress of the Old Testament is on the unity of God, in contrast to the degraded polytheism of the heathen nations. Although there are adumbrations of the Trinity in the Old Testament, this doctrine is clearly stated only in the New Testament. Again, there is progression from the recorded teaching of Jesus to the fuller understanding of His person and work which we find in the Epistles and the Prologue to the Fourth Gospel. But this is exactly what Jesus Himself led us to expect by what He said to the apostles in the upper room:

'I have yet many things to say to you, but you cannot bear them now. When the Spirit of truth comes, He will guide you into all the truth; for He will not speak on His own authority, but whatever He hears He will speak, and He will declare to you the things that are to come. He will glorify Me, for He will take what is Mine and declare it to you. All that the Father has is Mine; therefore I said that He will take what is Mine and declare it to you.'[1]

Progression is not the same as contradiction, however. An artist begins by making a sketch, and then applies his oils to the canvas bit by bit until the whole picture (present to his mind from the start, though not to the beholder's) finally emerges. Again, parents teach their children step by step, 'precept upon precept, precept upon precept, line upon line, line upon line, here a little, there a little'.[2] But if they are wise, they do not teach anything in the early stages which needs later to be contradicted. Their later teaching supplements what has gone before and builds on it; it does not come into collision with it. So God has gradually filled out His revelation, constantly expanding it but never repudiating it, until at last it was complete in Christ the Word made flesh (than whom a higher revelation is inconceivable) and in the witness of the apostles to Christ.

The Letter to the Hebrews opens with a very valuable statement of this truth:

'In many and various ways God spoke of old to our fathers by the prophets; but in these last days He has spoken to us by a Son . . .'[3]

Here the author concedes that there are several differences between the Old and New Testament revelations. The revelation was given at different times ('of old' and 'in these last days'), to different people ('to our fathers' and 'to us') and especially in different modes ('in many and various ways . . . by the prophets' and 'by a Son'). But though the occasion, the recipients and the manner of the revelation were different, its author was the same. It is *God* who spoke to the fathers in various ways through the prophets, and it is *God* who has spoken to us in and through His Son.

In the light of this we should not hesitate to claim God Himself as the ultimate author of both Testaments or to designate the whole of Scripture 'the Word of God'. (I discuss this further later in this book).

What, then, has God spoken? The Bible is essentially a revelation of God. It is, in fact, a divine self-disclosure. In the Bible we hear God speaking about God. To say this is not inconsistent with the thesis developed in the first chapter that the Bible is concerned with salvation and bears witness to Christ. For what God says about Himself is, above all else, that He has conceived and fulfilled a plan to save fallen men through Christ.

**The Living and Consistent God**
But before we come to His saving activity, there are two basic truths about Him to consider, which Scripture

3

emphasizes throughout. The first is that He is a living and sovereign God; the second that He is consistent, always the same, 'the Father of lights with whom there is no variation or shadow due to change'.[4]

Again and again the one, living and true God is contrasted with the dead idols of heathendom. Prophets and psalmists hold heathen idols up to ridicule. Isaiah describes the scene in one of the temples when Babylon was captured. He pictures the chief Babylonian deities being snatched ignominiously from their pedestals, carried out on men's shoulders and loaded on to carts outside. Fancy gods being carried by men and becoming 'burdens on weary beasts'! And when the laughter subsides, the voice of God is heard. He is no idol needing to be carried about by men, for it is He who carries His people:

'Hearken to Me, O house of Jacob,
all the remnant of the house of Israel,
who have been borne by Me from your birth, carried from the womb; even to your old age I am He, and to grey hairs I will carry you. I have made, and I will bear; I will carry and will save.'[5]

Not only the idols' inability to save aroused the prophets' scorn, but their total lifelessness:

'Their idols are silver and gold, the work of men's hands.
They have mouths, but do not speak; eyes, but do not see.
They have ears, but do not hear; noses, but do not smell.
They have hands, but do not feel; feet, but do not walk; and they do not make a sound in their throat.'[6]

4

In contrast to them, 'our God is in the heavens; He does whatever He pleases'.[7] He is the living God, who sees and hears and speaks and acts.

This living God is sovereign, a great king over all the earth. He is king of nature, and king of the nations also.

As king of nature He sustains the universe He has made and all its creatures. Even the ferocious elements are under His control. 'The sea is His, for He made it',[8] and the 'stormy wind' fulfils His command.[9] Psalm 29 gives a dramatic description of a thunderstorm, in which 'the voice of the Lord' breaks the cedars of Lebanon. The lightning flashes. The wilderness is shaken. The forests are stripped bare. The rain causes floods. As havoc spreads, one would expect apprehension and alarm to spread with it. But the psalmist remains quietly confident that God is in control:

'The Lord sits enthroned over the flood; the Lord sits enthroned as king for ever'.[10]

Psalm 104 is a primitive study in ecology. In it the psalmist marvels[11] at the way storks make their homes in firtrees, while 'the high mountains are for the wild goats' and 'the rocks are a refuge for the badgers' (i.e. the rock hyrax). The psalm goes on to describe how God feeds all animals:

'These all look to Thee, to give them their food in due season.
When thou givest to them, they gather it up;
when Thou openest Thy hand, they are filled with good things.'[12]

Entirely in keeping with this Old Testament insistence that God is the Lord of nature is the teaching of Jesus in the sermon on the mount, that God rules the animate and inanimate worlds. On the one hand He feeds the birds

5

of the air and clothes the lilies of the field; on the other 'He makes His sun rise on the evil and on the good, and sends rain on the just and on the unjust'.[13]

The king of nature is also king of nations. As Daniel said to King Nebuchadnezzar, 'the Most High rules the kingdom of men and gives it to whom He will'.[14] We saw in an earlier chapter how the little countries of Israel and Judah often seemed no more than pawns on an international chessboard. The great power blocks of the day were the empires of Egypt and Mesopotamia. As they confronted each other on the battlefield, and the tide of war ebbed and flowed, it was Israel and Judah and the small neighbouring states which got caught in between. Yet Israel continually uttered the splendid shout of faith:

'The Lord reigns; let the peoples tremble!'[15]

No power on earth, whether alone or in coalition with others, could triumph over God's people without God's permission. Do the nations scheme and plot, and set themselves against the Lord and against His anointed?

'He who sits in the heavens laughs; the Lord has them in derision.'[16]

The apostles of Jesus in New Testament days had the same conviction. When Peter and John were forbidden to speak or teach at all in the name of Jesus, they called their friends to prayer. They lifted their voices together to God as the 'sovereign Lord', the creator of the universe. Then they recited the first two verses of Psalm 2 (from which I have just quoted) and applied them to Herod and Pontius Pilate, the Gentiles and the rulers of Israel. These had conspired together in Jerusalem against Jesus. To do what? 'To do whatever Thy hand and Thy plan had predestined to take place.'[17]

6

More than that. The prophets taught that the mighty soldier-emperors of the day, some of whom were cruel and ruthless men, were yet instruments in the hand of the Lord. Shalmaneser of Assyria was the rod of His anger, the staff of His fury, with which to punish Samaria,[18] Nebuchadnezzar of Babylon His 'servant' through whom He would destroy Jerusalem[19] and Cyrus of Persia His 'anointed' to free His people from their captivity.[20]

If the God of the Bible is the living and the sovereign God, He is also always self-consistent. His sovereign power is never arbitrarily used. On the contrary, His activity is always consistent with His nature. One of the most important statements about God in Scripture is that 'He cannot deny Himself'.[21] Does it come as a surprise that it is said God 'cannot' do something? Can He not do anything? Is He not omnipotent? Yes, He can do anything He pleases to do, anything which it is consistent with His nature to do. But His omnipotence does not mean that He can do absolutely anything whatsoever; for He limits it by His own self-consistency.

God's love and wrath, together with His works of salvation and of judgment, are sometimes set over against each other as supposedly incompatible. We have already mentioned how some people imagine the God of the Old Testament to be a God of anger and the God of the New Testament to be a God of mercy. But this is a false antithesis. The Old Testament also reveals Him as a God of mercy, while the New Testament also reveals Him as a God of judgment. Indeed the whole Bible, Old and New Testaments alike, presents Him as a God of love and wrath simultaneously. The Biblical authors are not embarrassed by this, as many moderns seem to be. Thus, the apostle John can tell his readers how 'God so loved the world that He gave His only Son' and at the end of the same chapter declare that on him who does not obey the

Son 'the wrath of God rests'[22] Similarly, the apostle Paul can describe his readers as 'by nature the children of wrath, like the rest of mankind' and in the very next verse write that God is 'rich in mercy' and has loved us with a great love.[23]

The only explanation the Bible gives of the loving and wrathful activity of God, of His deeds of salvation and of judgment, is simply that He is like that. That is the kind of God He is, and this is why He acts that way. 'God is love', and therefore He loves the world and has given His Son for us.[24] But also 'our God is a consuming fire'.[25] His nature of perfect holiness can never compromise with evil but, as it were, 'devours' it. Always He sets Himself implacably against it.

One of the ways in which Scripture dares to express this truth of God's self-consistency is to say that He must and will 'satisfy Himself'.[26] That is to say, He is always perfectly Himself and acts in a way that is true to Himself. In every situation He expresses *Himself* as He is, in mercy and in judgment.

Having now drawn attention to the Biblical revelation of God as both living and sovereign on the one hand, and self-consistent on the other, there can be no doubt that the principal way in which the living God has expressed Himself is in 'grace'. No one can understand the message of Scripture, who does not know the meaning of grace. The God of the Bible is 'the God of all grace'.[27] Grace is love, but love of a special sort. It is love which stoops and sacrifices and serves, love which is kind to the unkind and generous to the ungrateful and undeserving. Grace is God's free and unmerited favour, loving the unlovable, seeking the fugitive, rescuing the hopeless, and lifting the beggar from the dunghill to make him sit among princes.[28]

It is grace which led God to establish His covenant with a particular people. God's grace is covenant grace.

True, it is also shown to everybody without distinction. This is called His 'common grace', by which He gives to all men indiscriminately such blessings as reason and conscience, love and beauty, life and food, marriage and children, work and leisure, ordered government and many other gifts besides. Yet God's entering into a special covenant with a special people may be described as His characteristic act of grace. For in it He took the initiative to choose out a people for Himself and to pledge Himself to be their God. He did not choose Israel because they were greater or better than other peoples. The reason for His choice lay in Him, not in them. As Moses explained it,

> 'The Lord has set His love upon you . . . because the Lord loves you'.[29]

'Covenant' is a legal term, and signifies any binding undertaking. When used in Scripture to describe what God has done, however, it is not to be thought of as an agreement between two equal parties, a kind of mutual contract. It is more like a 'testament' or will in which the testator has sole and entire discretion in the disposal of His own estate. Indeed, the English words 'covenant' and 'testament' can be used interchangeably, which is why the two halves of the Bible are known as the Old and New 'Testaments'. The Greek word *diathēkē* can mean either, and twice in the epistles there is a play on the two meanings of the word, in order to make it plain that God's covenant is like a 'last will and testament' in that He has freely made certain promises.[30] His covenant promises are not unconditional, since His people are required to obey His commands and this is their part of the covenant, but God Himself lays down the commands as well as the promises. So even at Sinai God's covenant remains a covenant of grace.

9

It is important to grasp, then, that the covenant of God is the same throughout, from Abraham to Christ, so that those who are Christ's by faith are thereby Abraham's children and heirs of the promises God made him.[31] The law which was given at Sinai did not annul the covenant of grace. On the contrary, the covenant of grace was confirmed and renewed at Sinai. What the law did was to emphasize and expand the requirement of obedience. It is only when the law is considered in isolation from the covenant of grace that it is contrasted with the gospel. Then the law is seen to condemn the sinner for his disobedience, while the gospel offers him life by grace.

We are now in a position to think about what may be described as three stages in the outworking of God's covenant, expressed in the three words 'redemption', 'adoption' and 'glorification'.

### Redemption

Redemption is originally not a theological but a commercial word. Often in the Old Testament (as today) we read about the redemption of land, which had been alienated from the owner's possession, or mortgaged. There were people also who needed to be redeemed, such as slaves and prisoners. In each case something or somebody was bought, in fact bought back from some state of alienation or bondage. To redeem was to purchase somebody's freedom, to recover by payment of a price something which had been lost.

This is the word which came to be applied to God's first act of grace towards His people. When they had somehow got lost, separated from Him and from their homeland in exile or captivity, He delivered them from their bondage and restored them to their land. This pattern repeated itself three times in Israel's history. First He called Abraham from Ur of the Chaldees (not, strictly speaking, a redemption because Abraham had not yet been in Canaan), then He delivered Israel from their Egyptian bondage and finally the exiles from their Babylonian captivity. In each He called, He acted, He delivered, and He brought them to the land of promise.

This is the Old Testament background to Jesus Christ's great work of redemption. Now man's alienation and bondage are spiritual. It is his sin—his rebellion against both his Creator's authority and his neighbour's welfare —which has enslaved him and separated him from God. And man in sin is man under judgment, deserving nothing for his revolt but death.

Into this situation of helplessness and despair came Jesus Christ. He took upon Him man's nature when He was born and man's guilt when He died. In the stark, unvarnished language of the New Testament He was first 'made flesh', and then 'made sin', even 'made a curse' for us.[32] For the simple truth is that He took our place. He identified Himself so completely with us in our predicament that He bore our sin and died our death. Our life was forfeit because of sin. He died instead of us, experiencing in our place the desolation of God-forsaken darkness.

The New Testament authors several times draw an analogy between the Passover, which initiated Israel's redemption from Egypt, and the death of Christ which has secured our redemption from sin. The life of every firstborn in Egypt was forfeit, but God made provision for the life of a lamb to be acceptable instead, if its blood was first shed and then sprinked on the lintel and side-posts of the front door. When God saw the blood, He passed over the house to protect it from His own judgment.

The New Testament fulfilment is dramatic. John showed in his Gospel that by one reckoning Jesus was

11

shedding His blood on the cross·at the precise time when the Passover lambs were being killed.[33] Paul wrote that 'Christ, our paschal (i.e. Passover) lamb, has been sacrificed',[34] while Peter referred to 'the precious blood of Christ, like that of a lamb without blemish or spot', which was shed to redeem us and must (symbolically, of course) be 'sprinkled' upon us.[35]

When Christ the Lamb of God had offered Himself as our Passover sacrifice, had shed his blood and died, God raised Him from the dead to vindicate Him, and to demonstrate that His sacrifice for sin had not been offered in vain. Now He is described as 'seated at God's right hand', resting from His finished work of redemption and crowned with glory and honour. He has won an 'eternal redemption'[36] for us. And throughout eternity the multitudes of heaven will sing 'Worthy is the Lamb who was slain . . .'[37]

### Adoption

Redemption is a largely negative concept. It concentrates on the plight from which we have been delivered and on the price which had to be paid. True, to be redeemed from sin by Christ's blood is to be redeemed 'for God'.[38] But this positive aspect of our salvation is emphasized rather in the notion of our adoption to be His children. Paul brings the two together as virtually inseparable when he writes:

> 'When the time had fully come, God sent forth His Son, born of woman, born under the law, to redeem those who were under the law, so that we might receive adoption as sons. . . . So through God you are no longer a slave but a son, and if a son then an heir.'[39]

Redeemed from slavery and adopted into sonship— that is the glorious double privilege of those who put

12

their trust in Christ. Our relationship to God as His children is an essential part of His covenant promise.

Already this fact of 'belonging to God' was plain in Old Testament days. The covenant formula, used each time the covenant was renewed, was 'I will be your God, and you shall be My people'. Moreover, this adoption of Israel to be the people of God immediately followed their redemption. Again and again God had to remind them of this, saying 'I am the Lord your God, who brought you out of the land of Egypt, out of the house of bondage'.[40] He had redeemed them. They were His. He spelled it out very clearly to them during the period between their redemption from Egypt and the renewal of the covenant at Sinai:

'You have seen what I did to the Egyptians, and how I bore you on eagles' wings and brought you to Myself. Now therefore, if you will obey My voice and keep My covenant, you shall be My own possession among all peoples; for all the earth is Mine, and you shall be to Me a kingdom of priests and a holy nation . . .'[41]

Often this covenant, by which God's redeemed people became His own possession, His special treasure, was likened to a marriage covenant. Yahweh was the husband of His people. He had delighted in His bride's early love and devotion in the wilderness.[42] But in Canaan she went after her 'lovers', the baals of the local shrines. She became an adulteress, even a harlot. She broke the covenant.

The marriage metaphor is continued and expanded in the New Testament. The apostle Paul described how 'Christ loved the church and gave Himself up for her', but added how anxious He was—imbued even with divine jealousy—lest this bride should be 'led astray from a sincere and pure devotion to Christ'.[43]

The relation between God and His people in New Testament days is expressed more often in terms of the

13

Father and his family, however, than of the husband and his wife. It is a development of the Old Testament conviction that Israel was God's 'firstborn son'.[44] Jesus regularly taught His disciples to regard God as their heavenly Father and themselves as His beloved children, to pray to Him as their Father, to trust His fatherly care to supply their material needs, and to become concerned for their Father's name, kingdom and will.

One of the greatest privileges of being God's children is to have the Holy Spirit dwelling within us. The personal and abiding presence of the Holy Spirit in our hearts is a distinctive blessing, distinctive both of the Christian era itself,[45] and of the individual Christian. It is 'because we are sons' that 'God has sent the Spirit of His Son into our hearts'.[46] Paul enlarges on this:

'For all who are led by the Spirit of God are sons of God. For you did not receive the spirit of slavery to fall back into fear, but you have received the spirit of sonship. When we cry, "Abba! Father!" it is the Spirit Himself bearing witness with our spirit that we are children of God . . .'[47]

So the life of God's children may be described as 'life in the Spirit'. It is a life lived under the direction and by the power of the Holy Spirit. He bears witness with our spirit that we are indeed God's children. As the 'Spirit of wisdom and of revelation' in our knowledge of Christ,[48] He also opens the eyes of our heart to know Him better. And He is the *Holy* Spirit, seeking to lead us into *holiness*, to make us like Christ.[49] He subdues the power of our flesh (or fallen nature) and causes to ripen in our character His fruit of 'love, joy, peace, patience, kindness, goodness, faithfulness, meekness and self-control'.[50]

The children of God together form His family, the church, enjoying a direct continuity with God's people

14

in Old Testament days. This Christian brotherhood transcends all racial and social barriers. It is hard for us to imagine how great was 'the dividing wall of hostility' between Jew and Gentile. But Christ broke it down, and Paul devoted much of his Ephesian letter to the theme that Jews and Gentiles share in Christ on equal terms, being fellow-citizens of God's kingdom and fellow-members of God's family.[51]

Another great contemporary rift in society existed between those who were slaves and those who were free. In the Roman empire slaves had no rights before the law; all the privileges belonged to the free. But when Paul led to Christ a runaway slave called Onesimus, he sent him back to his master Philemon, begging him to welcome him 'no longer as a slave but more than a slave, as a beloved brother'.[52] The social effects of the gospel were explosive.

To sum up this unity, this equality, of all the members of God's family, Paul wrote:

'There is neither Jew nor Greek, there is neither slave nor free, there is neither male nor female; for you are all one in Christ Jesus.'[53]

This people of God is a 'holy' people, that is, a distinct or separate people, set apart from the rest of mankind to belong to God. Therefore they are called to be what they are, to manifest in their character and conduct the holiness of their status or position. They are 'called to be holy', that is, called to be different from the secular world, and not to be conformed to its outlook or standards. 'You shall not do as they do', God had said to Israel in the wilderness, referring both to the Egyptians and to the Canaanites.[54] Similarly, 'do not be like them', Jesus said during the Sermon on the Mount, referring both to the Gentiles and to the Pharisees.

15

Instead, the Christian is to follow Christ. And His absolute ethical standards are set forth without compromise in both the Gospels and the Epistles, just as God's standards were set before Israel in the law and the prophets.

It must not be thought, however, that Christ's call to His people to be 'holy' or 'different' provides any excuse for withdrawal from the world into a pietistic isolation. On the contrary, the very same people whom Christ has 'chosen out of the world' He sends back 'into the world' as His representatives, to give themselves to other people in humble service and witness.[55]

Further, as they remain in the world for Christ, seeking to serve the world's needs but refusing to become assimilated to the world's standards, they will experience the world's opposition. The world will hate them for their very difference, Christ warned, and persecute them too.[56] So they will suffer. Indeed, to suffer unjustly and to forbear revenge is another part of the calling of Christians. For Christ left us an example of this, that we should follow in His footsteps.[57]

But suffering leads to glory. It was so for Christ. It is so for the followers of Christ. Peter commands us to rejoice both in our share of Christ's sufferings and in our anticipated share in the glory which is to be revealed.[58] The apostle Paul said the same thing:

'If children, then heirs, heirs of God and fellow-heirs with Christ, provided we suffer with Him in order that we may also be glorified with Him.'[59]

These are some of the implications of our 'adoption' into God's family. As children of our Father God, we are the dwelling place of His Spirit, united in brotherhood to all other Christian people, the ambassadors of Christ in the world, serving and suffering for His cause, and Christ's fellow-heirs as well.

16

For to be a son is to be an heir. Suffering is the pledge of glory. This leads us straight to the third stage in God's unfolding plan of salvation, 'glorification'.

## Glorification

The New Testament is full of the Christian hope. It reminds us that, although in the past we have been redeemed from sin by Christ and are now enjoying the privileges of sonship which adoption into God's family has brought us, there is still far more to come. To this consummation we are eagerly looking forward. For our Christian 'hope' has no uncertainty about it. It is a joyful and confident expectation, based upon the promises of God. And it sustains us as we travel like pilgrims to our eternal home.

What is the object of our hope? To what are we looking forward? Paul called it 'the hope of glory'.[60] But what does this mean?

First, the return of Christ. It is not fashionable to believe in this today, or not in any literal sense. But Jesus clearly and repeatedly said He was going to come back, and that His return would be 'in power and great glory'. The apostles enlarged on this assurance. His coming will be personal and visible, although it will also have a transcendent quality which puts it beyond our present understanding:

> 'For as the lightning comes from the east and shines as far as the west, so will be the coming of the Son of man.'[61]

Secondly, the resurrection. Resurrection is not the same as resuscitation. Those whom Jesus raised from death during His earthly ministry were resuscitated. They came back from death, resumed their former way of life, and then later died a second time. Resurrection, however, means the beginning of a new, a different, an

17

immortal life. So our resurrected bodies, though retaining some kind of continuity with our present bodies, will also be changed. They will be as different, Paul says, as the plant is from the seed out of which it grows. They will be set free both from decay and from 'the flesh', the fallen nature which in some sense belongs to them. They will also have new powers. In fact our resurrection body will be a 'body of glory', like Christ's.[62]

Thirdly, the judgment. When Christ comes, both salvation and judgment will be brought to completion. For both are processes begun in this life, as Jesus made plain.[63] We shall be judged according to our works.[64] We cannot be justified (brought into acceptance with God) by our works; justification is only by God's grace through faith in Christ and His finished work. But we shall be judged by our works, because the judgment will be a public occasion, and our 'works'—what we have said and done—will be the only public evidence which can be adduced to prove the presence (or absence) of any saving faith. Those whose works reveal that they have disobeyed the gospel and rejected Christ will be lost. Whatever its precise nature may be, hell is a terrible reality. Christ called it 'outer darkness' and told us to fear God 'who can destroy both soul and body in hell'.[65]

Fourthly, the new universe. It is variously described. There will be 'a new heaven and a new earth',[66] for God will 'make all things new'.[67] Jesus called it 'the rebirth',[68] Paul the heading up or uniting of all things in Christ[69] and Peter the 'restoration of all things.'[70]

Popular Christian devotion has perhaps concentrated too much on the negative joys of heaven, that is, on the promises of the Revelation that there will be no more hunger or thirst, no more scorching heat or sunstroke, no more tears or pain, no more night, no more curse, no more death. Thank God for these absences. But thank

18

God even more for their cause, namely the presence—
the central, dominating presence—of the throne of God.

When John was granted his vision of heavenly reality,
and was permitted to peer through 'an open door', the
first thing on which his eye rested was 'a throne',[71] the
symbol of God's sovereignty. Everything else in his vision
was related to this throne. The Father sat on it, and the
Lamb shared it, together with 'the seven spirits of God'
representing the Holy Spirit. Round it in concentric
circles were twenty-four elders symbolizing the church
and four living creatures symbolizing the creation, and
beyond them myriads of angels. Flashes of lightning and
peals of thunder issued from the throne, and before the
throne stood the great concourse of the redeemed,
drawn from every nation and language, wearing white
robes of righteousness, waving palm branches of victory,
and ascribing their salvation to their God who sits on the
throne and to the Lamb.[72]

The Bible begins with the creation of the universe and
ends with the re-creation of the universe. It goes on at its
beginning to describe the fall of man in a garden and
paradise lost; it concludes in a garden, with paradise
regained. Here are the tree of life for food and for healing,
and the water of life for refreshment. And the river of the
water of life is seen to be 'flowing from the throne of God
and of the Lamb.'[73] For at last God's kingdom has been
consummated. All creation is subject to Him. And the
blessings of our final inheritance will be due to His
perfect rule. So the great multitude sings:

'Hallelujah! For the Lord our God the Almighty
reigns.'[74]

And somehow His redeemed, adopted, glorified people
will share in His reign:

'They shall reign for ever and ever.'[75]

19

## For Further Reading

*The Message of the Old Testament* by H. L. Ellison (Paternoster 1969, 94 pages). Described as 'a primer to the understanding of the Old Testament *as a whole*', this book is written in the conviction that the Old and the New Testament are each incomplete without the other. After an initial chapter on 'the Problem of the Old Testament' the author takes us chronologically through the Hebrew Bible, unfolding the message of the historical books, the law, the prophets, the psalter and the wisdom literature. Concise, but thorough.

*A Day that Changed the World* by Gordon Bridger (Inter-Varsity Press 1975, 96 pages). Gordon Bridger outlines the New Testament teaching concerning the life, person, death and resurrection of Christ and attempts to assess the meaning of his death.

*A Summary of Christian Doctrine* by Louis Berkhof (1938, Banner of Truth edition 1960, 184 pages). Louis Berkhof, who died in 1957, came from a Dutch Reformed background and taught for many years at Calvin Theological Seminary, Grand Rapids, USA. His chapters on God, man, Christ, the application of redemption, the church and the last things are concise summaries of traditional reformed theology. Each chapter ends with questions both for review and for further study.

# NOTES

1 Jn. 16.12–15
2 Is. 28.10
3 Heb. 1.1–2
4 James 1.17
5 Is. 46.3, 4
6 Ps. 115.4–7
7 Ps. 115.3
8 Ps. 95.5
9 Ps. 148.8
10 Ps. 29.10
11 Ps. 104.17, 18
12 Ps. 104.27, 28
13 Mt. 5.45; 6.26–30
14 Dan. 4.32
15 Ps. 99.1
16 Ps. 2.4
17 Acts 4.18, 23–28
18 Is. 10.5, 6
19 Jer. 25.9; 27.6
20 Is. 45.1–4 cf. 44.28
21 2 Tim. 2.13
22 Jn. 3.16, 36
23 Eph. 2.3, 4
24 1 Jn. 4.8, 9
25 Heb. 12.19 quoting Dt. 4.24
26 For verses in which God says He will 'spend', 'satisfy' or 'give full vent to' His anger and thus judge His people for their inveterate rebellion, see e.g. Ezek. 5.13 ff; 6.12; 7.8; 16.42, 43; 24.13, 14 and Lam. 4.11. In Psalm 89.33 ff, however, it is His steadfast love according to His covenant promise and oath which directs Him. 'I will not . . . be false to My faithfulness,' He says (v. 33). Cf. the declaration in Is. 53.11 that the Lord's suffering servant, seeing the fruit of His soul's travail, will 'be satisfied'.
27 1 Pet. 5.10
28 Ps. 113.7, 8
29 Dt. 7.7, 8
30 Gal. 3.15–18; Heb. 9.15–18
31 Gal. 3.29
32 Jn. 1.14; 2 Cor. 5.21; Gal. 3.13
33 Jn. 13.1; 18.28
34 1 Cor. 5.7
35 1 Pet. 1.2, 18, 19
36 Heb. 9.12
37 Rev. 5.12
38 Rev. 5.9
39 Gal. 4.4–7
40 Ex. 20.2
41 Ex. 19.4–6
42 Jer. 2.2; 31.32
43 Eph. 5.25; 2 Cor. 11.2, 3
44 e.g. Ex. 4.22
45 Jer. 31.33
46 Gal. 4.6
47 Rom. 8.14–16
48 Eph. 1.17
49 2 Cor. 3.18
50 Gal. 5.16–23
51 Eph. 2.19

52 Philem. 16
53 Gal. 3.28
54 Lev. 18.1–5
55 Jn. 15.19; 17.15–19
56 Jn. 15.18–25; 17.14
57 1 Pet. 2.18–23
58 1 Pet. 4.13; 5.1, 10
59 Rom. 8.17
60 Rom. 5.2
61 Mt. 24.27
62 see Phil. 3.21 and 1 Cor. 15.35–57
63 Jn. 5.19–29

64 Mt. 16.27; Jn. 5.28,29; Rom. 2.6; Rev. 20.11–15
65 Mt. 10,28
66 2 Pet. 3.13; Rev. 21.1
67 Rev. 21.5
68 Mt. 19.28, literally
69 Eph. 1.10
70 Acts 3.21, literally
71 Rev. 4.1, 2
72 Rev. 4–7
73 Rev. 22.1
74 Rev. 19.6
75 Rev. 22.5

## THE AUTHORITY OF THE BIBLE

I tried in the previous section to summarize the message of the Bible, and in the previous books I have outlined the geographical and the historical setting within which this message was received and recorded. But is the Biblical message what it purports to be, a revelation from God? Can we trust the Bible?

This question is crucial and cannot be dodged. Vital issues are at stake. For one thing, the Bible claims (as we have seen) to be a book of salvation, to 'instruct us for salvation'. Therefore we must know whether the way of salvation it unfolds is true or false. The eternal destiny of men depends upon it.

For another thing, the church of today is confused. The non-Christian world is constantly being treated to the unedifying spectacle of Christians in discord and disagreement. Why is this? The primary cause of confusion in the church is the lack of an agreed authority. Ultimately, of course, the church should submit to the authority of Christ, its Lord. But is it possible that Christ intends to rule and reform His church by His word? May it be that His exhortation 'He who has an ear, let him hear what the Spirit says to the churches'[1] is an invitation to listen to *Scripture* through which the Spirit still speaks to the church?

For these two reasons at least our enquiry as to whether and why the Bible has authority is of great practical importance.

Yet it is also at variance with the contemporary mood. Strong anti-authoritarian tides are running. There is a prevalent revolt against all established authority, of both institutions and traditions. If we could demonstrate that the Bible has authority, many people would on that account be more ready to reject than to accept it. In addition, it is fashionable nowadays to indulge in a little religious syncretism, that is, to deny to every religion whatever exclusive elements it may claim, to assert that all religions are relatively true and so to try to combine them. Other religions also have their holy books; what is so special about the Christian Scriptures, the Bible?

### Three Definitions

Aware, then, of the importance of our subject and of the disfavour with which many will regard our attempt to defend the uniqueness of the Bible, we shall begin with some definitions. The three great words commonly used by Christians in this connection are 'revelation', 'inspiration' and 'authority'. They are related but distinct.

The fundamental word is 'revelation'. Derived from a Latin noun meaning 'unveiling', it indicates that God has taken the initiative to make Himself known. The reasonableness of this concept should be plain. For whoever or whatever God may be, He is altogether beyond our ken. 'Can you find out the deep things of God? Can you find out the limit of the Almighty?'.[2] Indeed, not. His infinite greatness is veiled from our eyes. We cannot discover Him by ourselves. If we are ever to know Him, He must make Himself known.

The second word 'inspiration' indicates the chief mode God has chosen by which to reveal Himself. He has revealed Himself partly in nature and supremely in Christ, but also by 'speaking' to particular people. And it is this process of verbal communication which is called 'inspiration'. We do not use it in the general sense that we may say a poet or musician is 'inspired'. On the contrary, it has a special and precise connotation. For when Paul writes that 'all Scripture is inspired by God',[3] the last three words represent a single Greek expression which would be literally translated 'God-breathed'. The meaning, then, is not that God breathed into the writers, nor that He somehow breathed into the writings to give them their special character, but that what was written by men was breathed out by God. He spoke through them. They were His spokesmen.

Further, we do not hesitate to say that this inspiration was 'verbal inspiration', in that it extended to the very words used by the human authors. This is what they claimed. The apostle Paul, for example, could declare that in communicating to others what God had revealed to him, he used 'words not taught by human wisdom but taught by the Spirit'.[4] Nor is this in the least surprising, for it is not possible to convey a precise message in any other way than in precise words.

'Authority', the third word, is the power or weight which inheres in Scripture because of what it is, namely a divine revelation given by divine inspiration. If it is a word from God, it has authority over men. For behind every word that anybody utters stands the person who speaks it. It is the speaker himself (his character, knowledge and position) who determines how people regard his words. So God's word carries God's authority. It is because of who He is that we believe what He has said.

This is the lesson Simon Peter learned when Jesus told him on the lake of Galilee to put out into the deep and let down his nets for a catch. All his fisherman's expertise, gathered from years of experience, rebelled against the suggestion. He even protested, 'Master, we toiled all night and took nothing!'. Yet wisely he added 'But at Your word I will let down the nets.'[5]

Our claim, then, is that God has revealed Himself by speaking; that this divine (or God-breathed) speech has been written down and preserved in Scripture; and that Scripture is, in fact, God's word written, which therefore is true and reliable and has divine authority over men.

## Three Disclaimers

It seems necessary now to add to these definitions certain disclaimers which may anticipate objections and disarm possible criticism.

First, the process of inspiration was not a mechanical one. God did not treat the human authors of Scripture as dictating machines or tape recorders, but as living and responsible persons. Sometimes He spoke to them in dreams and visions, sometimes by an audible voice, sometimes by angels. At other times we are not told how the word of God came to them. They may well not have been conscious of it at all. Thus in the case of Luke the evangelist divine inspiration was certainly not incompatible with human research, for he tells us in the preface to his Gospel about the painstaking enquiries he had pursued. Whatever means of communication God employed in speaking to men, it never obliterated their own personality. On the contrary, as they wrote, their literary style and vocabulary were their own. So too—more important still—was their theme. It is not an accident that Amos was the prophet of God's justice, Hosea of His love and Isaiah of His kingly sovereignty, nor that Paul was the apostle of grace and faith, James of works, John of love, and Peter of hope. The internal evidence, culled from reading the Biblical text, is that God made full use of the personality, temperament, background and experience of the Biblical authors, in order to convey through each an appropriate and distinctive message.

So then Scripture is equally the word of God and the word of men. This is, indeed, how it describes itself. If it is true that 'the mouth of the Lord has spoken,'[6] it is also true that 'God spoke by the mouth of his holy prophets.'[7] Similarly, 'God spoke ... through the prophets,[8] and 'men ... spoke from God'.[9] Again, the law could be described by the same author in the same passage as both 'the law of Moses' and 'the law of the Lord'.[10]

The dual authorship of Scripture is an important truth to be carefully guarded. On the one hand, *God* spoke, revealing the truth and preserving the human authors from error, yet without violating their personality. On the other hand, *men* spoke, using their own faculties freely, yet without distorting the divine message. Their words were truly their own words. But they were (and still are) also God's words, so that what Scripture says, God says.

My second disclaimer is that, although Scripture as God's word is true, this does not mean—to quote a common claim—that 'every word of the Bible is literally true.' Such a statement would need to be qualified in several ways. Although I am here trespassing slightly upon what I write in Book 5 about Biblical interpretation, I think I need to say something about it here.

To begin with, every word of the Bible is true only in its context. Isolated from its context, it may be quite untrue. The best example of what I mean is the Book of

Job, the bulk of which consists of a dialogue between the grief-stricken Job and his three 'comforters', together with a fourth who appears later. This occupies chapters 1 to 37. Then God reveals Himself to Job in chapters 38 to 42. Some of what Job and his comforters say about suffering in the first 37 chapters is mistaken. It is recorded in order to be contradicted, not in order to be believed. We are told so at the end of the book when Job says to God 'I have uttered what I did not understand' and God says to his comforters 'you have not spoken of Me what is right.'[11] It would be quite impossible, therefore, to take any verse from the Book of Job and say 'this is the word of God', for it may not be. The book as a whole is God's word, but the first 37 chapters can be understood only in the light of the last 5.

Then again much of Scripture is deliberately presented in a highly figurative manner. Thus, there are many 'anthropomorphic' descriptions of God, representing Him in human form, and referring to His eyes and ears, His 'outstretched arm', 'mighty hand' and fingers, His mouth, His breath and His nostrils. We do not interpret these *literally*, for the simple reason that 'God is spirit'[12] and therefore has no body. So when we read that 'the eyes of the Lord run to and fro throughout the whole earth, to show His might in behalf of those whose heart is blameless toward Him,'[13] we do not try to visualize a pair of divine eyes running about over the earth's surface, but understand rather that God sees everyone everywhere and is always ready to save those who trust in Him. In the same way, when we read of people hiding under His 'wings', we do not picture Him as a bird with feathers, but learn that He protects those who take refuge in Him.

Similarly, when the Psalmist writes that the sun 'comes forth like a bridegroom leaving his chamber, and like a strong man runs its course with joy', and when he goes on to refer to the sun's 'rising' and 'circuit' from one end

28

of the heavens to the other,[14] he does not commit us to a pre-Copernican view of the solar system. For he is evidently describing the sun's resplendent magnificence both in poetic imagery and from the point of view of an earth-bound observer. Even sophisticated technocrats of the 1970s can wax eloquent about the sun, and can talk of its 'rising' and 'setting'. They do not need to apologize for doing so. Men recognize that they are using the language of poetry, and of ordinary observation, not of science.

The third disclaimer I would make concerns what the inspired text of Scripture is, which alone can be regarded as God's word written. This is the original Hebrew or Greek text as it came from the authors' hands. We claim no special inspiration or authority for any particular translation—whether ancient Latin or modern English, nor indeed for any particular interpretation.

It is true that no actual autograph has survived. Their loss is presumably due to a deliberate providence of God, which may have been to prevent men giving superstitious reverence to pieces of paper. Nevertheless, we know something of the scrupulous care with which scribes copied the sacred Hebrew text, and the same will have been true of the New Testament documents. Further, we possess far more early copies of the original text than of any other ancient literature. By comparing these with each other, with the early 'versions' (i.e. translations) and with Biblical quotations in the writings of the church fathers, scholars (so called 'textual critics') have been able to establish the authentic text (especially of the New Testament) beyond any reasonable doubt. The uncertainties which remain are almost entirely trivial; no doctrine of any importance hangs upon them.

So far I have tried to clear the ground by indicating both what we do and what we do not claim for the Bible. It is now time to ask on what grounds we base our assurance that it is God's word written, originating with God and authoritative for men. Many different answers have been given. I will touch on the first three briefly and concentrate on the fourth and decisive argument.

### Arguments for the Authority of Scripture

The first point to make is that the historic Christian churches have consistently maintained and defended the divine origin of Scripture. Only in comparatively recent times have some churches changed their official doctrine on this matter. Whether we consult the formularies of Roman, Anglican, Presbyterian, Lutheran or other churches, the witness is virtually unanimous. Now this is not a conclusive argument and may not appeal at all to some. Nevertheless, the tradition of the centuries is not to be lightly set aside or despised, and the consensus on this matter is very impressive.

Secondly, we turn from what the historic churches have consistently taught to what the Biblical writers themselves claimed. This is even more impressive. For example, Moses said he received the law from God. The prophets introduced their oracles with formulae like 'Thus says the Lord' or 'The word of the Lord came to me, saying'. And the apostles could write such statements as this one from Paul:

> 'When you received the word of God which you heard from us, you accepted it not as the word of men but as what it really is, the word of God, which is at work in you believers.'[15]

The Biblical authors also made similar claims for each other. We find in Scripture an elaborate pattern of cross-authorization. For example, the prophets endorsed the law, and the psalmists extolled its truth, beauty and sweetness.[16] Above all, the New Testament confirms the

Old, the apostolic authors drawing from it a rich variety of quotations as divine warrant for what they were writing. There is even the famous passage in which the apostle Peter refers to the letters of 'our beloved brother Paul,' comments on the 'wisdom' given to him and equates his epistles with Scripture.[17]

The third line of evidence for the inspiration and authority of Scripture is supplied not by the writers but by the readers of Scripture. For there are certain characteristics of the Bible which cannot fail to strike the observant reader. There is, for instance, the book's remarkable unity and coherence, on which I have tried to enlarge in earlier chapters. In view of the diversity of human authorship, the best explanation of this unity seems to be the overshadowing activity of a single divine author behind the human authors. There is also, as one aspect of this overall unity, the striking phenomenon of fulfilled prophecy. Then there are the nobility and dignity of the great themes of Scripture and the extraordinary relevance of its message thousands of years later, to which its continuing popularity bears witness.

Further, there is the power which the Bible has had (God's power through it, we believe) in human lives, disturbing the complacent and comforting the sorrowful, abasing the proud, reforming the sinful, encouraging the faint-hearted, bringing hope to the bereaved and giving direction to those who have lost their way. Added to all this is what the Reformers called 'the inward witness of the Holy Spirit'. It is the deep assurance that Scripture is truth from God, an assurance arising not from external confirmation such as archaeological discoveries (helpful as these are), but internally from the Holy Spirit Himself. It is the experience of the 'burning heart', given first to the disciples on the Emmaus Road, but still granted to Christian disciples of the modern world:

31

'Did not our hearts burn within us while He talked to us on the road, while He opened to us the Scriptures.'[18]

However, the first and foremost reason why Christians believe in the divine inspiration and authority of Scripture is not because of what the churches teach, the writers claimed or the readers sense, but because of what Jesus Christ Himself said. Since He endorsed the authority of Scripture, we are bound to conclude that His authority and Scripture's authority either stand or fall together.[19]

Some may at once retort that to rely on Christ's witness to Scripture is to employ a circular argument, which might be expressed like this: 'How do I know that Scripture is inspired? Because of Christ, who says so. How do I know that Christ says so? Because of Scripture, which is inspired.' This, our critics point out, is to beg the question. For it is to assume the very truth we are wanting to prove. But they have misstated our argument. When we make our first approach to the Bible, we bring with us no assumptions about its divine inspiration. We accept it merely as a collection of historical documents, containing in particular the witness of first century Christians to Christ. As we read their testimony, we come to believe in Christ, still without formulating any particular doctrine of Scripture. But then the Christ we have come to believe in sends us back to Scripture. He gives us a new understanding of it because He endorses its authority for us.

But how did Christ endorse Scripture? Scripture consists, of course, of two separate halves, the Old and the New Testaments. And the way in which Jesus Christ set His seal on each is different.


### Christ's view of the Old Testament

Take the Old Testament first. There can be no doubt, as any careful readers of the Gospels will agree, that Jesus gave His reverent assent to the authority of Old Testament Scripture, for He submitted to its authority Himself. I will give three examples to demonstrate this.

First, Jesus submitted to the Old Testament in His personal conduct. Thus, He countered each of the temptations of the devil by an apt Biblical quotation. It is sometimes said that He quoted Scripture 'at the devil'. This is not so. It would be more accurate to say that He quoted Scripture at Himself in the presence of the devil. For when the devil offered Him the kingdoms of the world if He would fall down and worship him, Jesus replied:

'Begone, Satan! For it is written, "You shall worship the Lord your God and Him only shall you serve" '.[20]

Jesus was not applying this text to Satan, but to Himself. He knew from Scripture that worship was due to God alone. Therefore He would obey. As man He would worship God, not Satan. The simple word *gegraptai* ('it stands written') was enough for Him. There was no need to question, discuss, argue or negotiate. The matter had already been settled by Scripture. This voluntary, personal submission of God's Son to the authority of God's word is extremely significant.

Secondly, Jesus submitted to the Old Testament in the fulfilment of His mission. He seems to have come to an understanding of His Messianic role from a study of Old Testament Scripture. He knew Himself to be both Isaiah's suffering servant and Daniel's son of man. So He accepted that He could enter into His glory only by the road of suffering and death. This explains the sense of necessity, of compulsion which constrained Him:

'The son of man must suffer many things and be rejected . . . and be killed, and after three days rise again.'[21]

Why '*must*'? Because the Scripture said so. Voluntarily and deliberately He put Himself under the authority of what stood written, and He determined to fulfil it, in His mission as in His conduct. So when Peter tried to avert His arrest in the Garden of Gethsemane, He told Peter to sheathe his sword. He had no need of human defence. Could He not appeal to His Father for legions of defending angels? Then why did He not do so? Here is the reason He gave:

'How then should the Scriptures be fulfilled, that it must be so?'[22]

He was of the same opinion after the resurrection, and confirmed it both to the two Emmaus disciples and to the wider group of His followers:

'Was it not necessary that the Christ should suffer these things and enter into His glory? These are My words which I spoke to you, while I was still with you, that everything written about Me in the law of Moses and the prophets and the psalms must be fulfilled.'[23]

Thirdly, Jesus submitted to the Old Testament in His controversies. He found Himself engaged in continuous debate with the religious leaders of His day, and whenever there was a difference of opinion between them, He regarded Scripture as the only court of appeal. 'What is written in the law?' He would ask. 'How do you read?'[24] Again, 'Have you not read this Scripture. . . . ?'[25] One of His chief criticisms of His contemporaries concerned their disrespect for Scripture. The Pharisees added to it and the Sadducees subtracted from it. So to the Pharisees He said:

'You have a fine way of rejecting the commandment of God, in order to keep your tradition! . . . making void the word of God through your tradition which you hand on.'[26]

And to the Sadducees:

'Is not this why you are wrong, that you know neither the Scriptures nor the power of God?'[27]

It is beyond question, then, that Jesus Christ was Himself personally submissive to Scripture. In His own ethical standards, in His understanding of His mission, and in debate with the Jewish leaders, what the Scripture said was decisive for Him. 'Scripture cannot be broken', He affirmed.[28] And again,

'Truly, I say to you, till heaven and earth pass away, not an iota, not a dot, will pass from the law until all is accomplished.'[29]

There is no example of Christ contradicting the divine origin of Old Testament Scripture. Some people have supposed that He did so in the six antitheses of the Sermon on the Mount, in which He said 'You have heard that it was said . . ., but I say to you . . .'. However, it is not Moses with whom He was at odds, but the scribal perversions of Moses; not Scripture (which is God's word), but tradition (which is man's). All the available evidence confirms that Jesus Christ assented in His mind and submitted in His life to the authority of Old Testament Scripture. Is it not inconceivable that His followers should have a lower view of it than He?

## Christ's Provision for the New Testament

Christ's way of endorsing the New Testament was, of course, different from His way of endorsing the Old, for none of the books of the New Testament had yet been written. If then the writing of the New Testament belonged entirely to the future, how could He endorse it at all?

The answer to this question lies in His appointment of the apostles. Jesus seems to have foreseen the need for Scriptures of the New Testament corresponding to the Scriptures of the Old. In the Old Testament God was active in redeeming and judging Israel, and Himself raised up prophets to give a true record and interpretation of what He was doing. Now God was active, through Christ, in redeeming and judging the world. Was this supreme and final revelation of God in Christ to be lost to future generations? No, there must be authoritative scribes and interpreters for this revelation as well. So Jesus made provision for this very thing. He carefully (after a whole night of prayer) chose and appointed, and then went on to train and authorize, the twelve apostles to be His witnesses, as God had chosen the prophets in Old Testament days:

> 'In those days He went out into the hills to pray; and all night He continued in prayer to God. And when it was day, He called His disciples, and chose from them twelve, whom He named apostles.'[30]

All the followers of Jesus were 'disciples'; only the twelve were named 'apostles'. A study of the New Testament use of the title shows that, although there were 'apostles of the churches' roughly equivalent to modern missionaries,[31] 'the apostles of Christ' were a small and restricted circle consisting of the Twelve, Matthias (who replaced Judas), Paul, James the Lord's brother, and perhaps one or two others. Although the whole church is apostolic in the sense that Christ sends it into the world on His mission, and although every Christian should be involved in this mission, yet 'apostle' is not a general word for a Christian in the New Testament. Even Paul's loyal and trusted colleagues like Timothy were not apostles. He deliberately drew a distinction between himself and them. Thus, he began his

36

letter to the Colossians: 'Paul, an apostle of Christ Jesus by the will of God, and Timothy our brother'. Timothy was a brother. Indeed, all Christians are brothers. But he was not an apostle of Christ like Paul.

Modern research suggests that the Greek word *apostolos* is the equivalent of the Aramaic *shaliach*, and that the *shaliach* in Rabbinic Judaism was a person with a clearly defined role. He was an emissary of the Sanhedrin, sent out to the Jews of the dispersion to teach in the Council's name. It was said of him: 'the one sent by a person is as this person himself'. In other words, he was a plenipotentiary, speaking with the authority of the person or body that had commissioned him. Thus Saul of Tarsus went to the synagogues at Damascus, armed 'with the authority and commission of the chief priests'.[32]

It is against this background that Jesus chose twelve men and deliberately gave them this title. The apostles were to be His personal representatives, endowed with His authority to speak in His name. When He sent them out, He said to them, 'He who receives you receives Me.'[33]

The apostles of Jesus appear to have had a fourfold uniqueness.

First, they had a personal call and authorization by Christ. This was clear in the case of the Twelve, and Paul claimed something comparable. He vehemently asserted and defended his apostolic authority, insisting that he had received his commission to be an apostle 'not from men nor through man, but through Jesus Christ and God the Father'.[34] It is further significant that in one of the accounts of Paul's conversion which Luke gives in the Acts, we are told the very words which Jesus used to commission him, namely *ego apostello se*, 'I send you' or 'I make you an apostle.'[35]

Secondly, they had an eye-witness experience of Christ. The twelve were appointed, Mark says, 'to be with Him,

37

and to be sent out to preach'.[36] The verb 'sent out' is again *apostellein*, and their essential qualification for the work of apostleship was to be 'with Him'. Similarly, shortly before He died, Jesus said to them:

'You also are witnesses, because you have been with Me from the beginning.'[37]

So He gave them unrivalled opportunities to hear His words and see His works, so that they might later bear witness to what they had seen and heard.[38] Especially was it important for them to be witnesses of His resurrection. It was for this that Matthias was chosen, 'to take the place in this ministry and apostleship from which Judas turned aside'.[39]

It is true, of course, that Paul was not one of the original twelve, that he did not have the eye-witness experience of Christ which they had, and that probably he never even saw Christ in the flesh. Some have conjectured that the three years he spent in Arabia, during which he says he received his gospel 'through a revelation of Jesus Christ',[40] were deliberately intended to compensate him for the three years of Christ's public ministry which he had missed. Be that as it may, he fulfilled this second apostolic qualification by being a witness of the resurrection. 'Am I not an apostle?' he cried; 'have I not seen Jesus our Lord?'[41] His reference is of course to his encounter with Christ on the Damascus Road. Although it took place after the Ascension, nevertheless he claims that it was an actual, objective resurrection appearance, and he adds that it was the last. At the end of his catalogue of the resurrection appearances he writes:

'Last of all, as to one untimely born, He appeared also to me. For I am the least of the apostles . . .'[42]

Thirdly, they had an extraordinary inspiration of the Holy Spirit. We saw in the previous chapter that the indwelling and illumination of the Holy Spirit is the privilege of all God's children. This privilege was not restricted to the apostles. Nevertheless, the ministry of the Spirit which Christ promised the apostles was something quite unique, as should be clear from these words:

'These things I have spoken to you, while I am still with you. But the Counsellor, the Holy Spirit, whom the Father will send in My name, He will teach you all things, and bring to your remembrance all that I have said to you. . . .
'I have yet many things to say to you, but you cannot bear them now. When the Spirit of truth comes, He will guide you into all the truth . . .'[43]

These wonderful promises have sometimes been applied to all Christian people. Doubtless they do have a secondary reference to us all. But their primary reference is evidently to the apostles who were gathered round Christ in the Upper Room, of whom He could say 'These things I have spoken to you while I am still with you' and 'I have yet many things to say to you, but you cannot bear them now.'

What He promised them was twofold. First, that the Holy Spirit would remind them of the teaching He had given them, and secondly that He would supplement it, leading them into all the truth which they could not at the moment bear. The major fulfilment of these promises was in the writing of the gospels and the epistles of the New Testament.

Fourthly, they had the power to work miracles. The Book of Acts is rightly called 'The Acts of the Apostles',[44] and Paul designates the 'signs and wonders and mighty works' which he had performed 'the signs of a true apostle'.[45] Further, the purpose of the miraculous power given to the apostles was to authenticate their apostolic commission and message:

39

'How shall we escape if we neglect such a great salvation? It was declared at first by the Lord (i.e. the Lord Jesus), and it was attested to us by those who heard Him (i.e. the apostolic eye-witnesses), while God also bore witness by signs and wonders and various miracles and by gifts of the Holy Spirit distributed according to His own will.'[46]

In these four ways the apostles seem to have been unique.

## The Apostles' Authority Confirmed

Our impression of the uniqueness of the apostles is confirmed in two ways. First, they themselves knew it, and so exhibit in the New Testament their self-conscious apostolic authority. This is certainly so of Paul and John. Paul not only defends his authority as an apostle (as we have seen); he asserts it. Listen to the dogmatic instructions he gave the Thessalonian Church:

'We have confidence in the Lord about you, that you are doing and will do the things which we command. ... Now we command you, brethren, in the name of our Lord Jesus Christ ... For even when we were with you, we gave you this command ... Now such persons we command and exhort in the Lord Jesus Christ. ... If anyone refuses to obey what we say in this letter ...'[47]

Who is this 'we'? It is the plural of apostolic authority. And who is it who presumes to issue these authoritative commands and to demand obedience? Again, it is an apostle of Christ, who speaks in the name of Christ. He claims that Christ was speaking in and through him.[48] As a result, when he first visited Galatia, although he was disfigured by illness, the Galatians did not scorn or despise him, but actually received him 'as an angel of God, as Christ Jesus'.[49] Paul does not rebuke them for paying him an exaggerated deference. On the contrary, they were right to receive him thus, for he was an apostle, an ambassador, an authorized representative of Jesus Christ.

John also used the plural of apostolic authority[50] and constantly recalled his readers to the original teaching he had given them. In view of the prevalence of false teachers he dared even to write:

'We are of God. Whoever knows God listens to us, and he who is not of God does not listen to us. By this we know the spirit of truth and the spirit of error.'[51]

In other words, a safe test by which John's readers could discern between truth and error was whether it was in accord with his teaching. False teachers would show their falsity by not listening to John, while the true Christian would authenticate himself by his submission to the apostle's authority.

The second way in which the unique authority of the apostles is substantiated is that the early church recognized it. For example, in the post-apostolic period, round about 110 A.D., soon after John the last apostle had died, Bishop Ignatius of Antioch sent letters to several churches of Asia Minor and Europe. In his *Epistle to the Romans* (ch. 4), he wrote:

'I do not, as Peter and Paul, issue commandments unto you. They were apostles; I am but a condemned man.'

He was a bishop. But he recognized that even a bishop's authority was not comparable to an apostle's.

When in the fourth century the church came finally to settle which books should be included in the New Testament canon and which excluded, the test they applied

41

was whether a book came from the apostles. That is, was it written by an apostle? If not, did it emanate from the circle of the apostles and carry the endorsement of their authority? It is important to add this, for not every New Testament book was written by an apostle. But it seems to have been recognized that if a non-apostolic document nevertheless carried a kind of apostolic imprimatur, it should be recognized as 'apostolic'. For example, Luke was known to have been a regular companion and colleague of Paul, and Mark was described by the early church fathers Papias and Irenaeus as 'the interpreter of Peter' who faithfully recorded Peter's memories of Christ and the substance of his preaching.[52] Thus, the church was in no sense conferring authority on the canonical books; it was simply recognizing the authority they already possessed.

It is time now to summarize the argument which has been developed. Christ endorsed the authority of the Old Testament. He also made provision for the New Testament by authorising His apostles to teach in His name. Therefore if we would bow to Christ's authority, we must bow to Scripture's. It is because of Jesus Christ that Christians submit to both Old and New Testaments.

What are the alternatives to this conclusion? There are only two.

The first is to say that Christ was mistaken in His view of Scripture. In this case the argument would run somewhat as follows: 'The incarnation imprisoned Jesus in the limited mentality of a first-century Jew. Of course He accepted the authority of Scripture, for this is what the Jews of His day believed. But that is no reason why we should. Their view and His are outmoded'. This is the so-called theory of 'kenosis', from the Greek word which declares that He 'emptied Himself'[53] when He became man. He certainly emptied Himself of His glory when He took the form of a servant. But He did not empty

Himself of His deity in becoming man. And although as man He seems to have been ignorant of certain matters (He said He did not know the day of His return[54]), the remarkable fact is that He was not ignorant of His ignorance. He knew the limits of His knowledge. Consequently in His instruction He never strayed beyond these limits. On the contrary, He insisted that He taught only what the Father gave Him to teach.[55] Therefore we claim that He was inerrant, that all His teaching was true, including His endorsement of the authority of Scripture.

The second alternative which has been proposed may be expressed like this: 'Jesus knew perfectly well that Scripture was not entirely the word of God and reliable. Yet because His contemporaries all believed that it was, He accommodated Himself to their position. There is no need for us to do so.' But this suggestion is quite intolerable. It is derogatory to Christ, and incompatible with His claim to be the truth, and teach the truth. Besides, He never hesitated to disagree with His contemporaries on other matters, so why should He have done so on this? Further, this reconstruction would attribute to Jesus the very thing He detested most—religious pretense, or hypocrisy.

So we reject both the 'kenosis' and the 'accommodation' theories. Over against them we must insist that Jesus knew what He was talking about, and that He meant it. He taught knowledgeably, deliberately and with entire sincerity. He declared the divine origin of all Scripture for the straightforward reason that He believed it. And what He believed and taught is true.

## Some Conclusions

In conclusion, let me emphasize both the rightness and the reasonableness of submitting to the authority of Scripture.

43

First, to accept the authority of the Bible is a Christian thing to do. It is neither a religious eccentricity, nor a case of discreditable obscurantism, but the good sense of Christian faith and humility. It is essentially 'Christian' because it is what Christ Himself requires of us. The traditional view of Scripture (that it is God's word written) is the Christian view of Scripture precisely because it is Christ's view of Scripture.

Secondly, what shall we do with the problems? To accept the divine origin of the Bible is not to pretend that there are no problems. To be candid, there are many problems—literary, historical, theological and moral. So what shall we do with them? Is it compatible with intellectual integrity to accept the unique authority of Scripture when so many residual problems surround it? Yes indeed it is.

We need to learn to do with the problems surrounding Scripture exactly what we do with the problems surrounding any other Christian doctrine. Every Christian doctrine has its problems. No doctrine is entirely free of them. Take as an example the doctrine of the love of God. Every Christian of every conceivable hue believes that God is love—Roman, Orthodox, Anglican, Reformed, Lutheran, Baptist, Brethren. It is a fundamental Christian doctrine. To disbelieve this is to disqualify oneself as a Christian. But the problems surrounding the doctrine are massive. What, then, do we do when someone brings us a problem touching God's love, a problem of evil or of undeserved suffering, for instance? In the first place, we shall wrestle with the problem and we may be granted some fresh light on it. But we are not likely to solve it altogether. So then what? Must we abandon our belief in the love of God until we have solved all the problems? No. We shall maintain our belief in the love of God, in spite of the problems, for one reason and for one reason only, namely that Jesus Christ taught it and exhibited it. That is why we believe that God is love. And the problems do not overthrow our belief.

So with Scripture. Someone brings us a problem, maybe an apparent discrepancy or a question of literary criticism. What shall we do? To begin with, we shall wrestle with the problem, and perhaps find fresh light on it. But we may well not entirely solve it. So then what? Must we abandon our belief in the Word of God until we have solved all the problems? No. We shall maintain our belief in God's Word, just as we maintain our belief in God's love, in spite of the problems, ultimately for one reason and for one reason only, namely that Jesus Christ taught it and exhibited it. It is no more obscurantist to cling to the one belief than the other. Indeed, it is not obscurantist at all. To follow Christ is always sober, humble, Christian realism.

Thirdly, the ultimate issue in the question of authority concerns the lordship of Christ. 'You call Me Teacher and Lord', He said, 'and you are right; for so I am'.[56] If Jesus Christ is truly our teacher and our lord, we are under both His instruction and His authority. We must therefore bring our mind into subjection to Him as our teacher and our will into subjection to Him as our lord. We have no liberty to disagree with Him or to disobey Him. So we bow to the authority of Scripture because we bow to the authority of Christ.

**For Further Reading**

*Is the Bible the Word of God?* by W. Graham Scroggie (Moody Press 1922, 123 pages). This reprint of a study by a well-loved author of an earlier generation provides a well-organized apologetic which covers external, internal and experimental evidence.

*This Is That* by F. F. Bruce (Paternoster 1968, 114 pages). A thoughtful, stimulating account of the way in which the New Testament Church offered a fresh presentation and interpretation of the Old Testament in the light of the Christ event. Subjects like the rule, salvation and victory of God are considered, together with the types of Messianic hope. Plenty of footnotes in this well-documented work encourage the reader to further study

*Basic Bible Studies* by Francis A. Schaeffer (Hodder and Stoughton 1973, 95 pages). The well-known founder and director of the L'Abri Fellowship has drawn up a study series of 25 basic Bible doctrines to provide a reasonably comprehensive understanding of the total teaching of Scripture. It is not meant to be read by itself but studied in conjunction with the Bible.

*The New Testament Documents: Are They Reliable?* by F. F. Bruce (IVF first published 1943, 122 pages). Professor Bruce is concerned in this paperback rather with the historical reliability of the New Testament, than with its theological truth. Alongside general chapters on dating, attestation, archaeology and external evidence, he has more specific chapters on the canon, the miracles, the Gospels and the writings of Paul and Luke. An invaluable summary.

## NOTES

1 Rev. 2 and 3
2 Job 11.7
3 2 Tim. 3.16
4 1 Cor. 2.13
5 Lk. 5.4, 5
6 e.g. Is. 1.20
7 e.g. Acts 3.21
8 Heb. 1.1
9 2 Pet. 1.21
10 Lk. 2.22, 23
11 Job 42.3, 7

12 Jn. 4.24
13 2 Chron. 16.9
14 Ps. 19.1–6
15 1 Thess. 2.13
16 e.g. Ps. 19 and 119
17 2 Pet. 3. 15, 16
18 Lk. 24.32
19 For a fuller treatment of this theme see the author's chapter 2 in *Guidelines* (Falcon 1967),

entitled 'Jesus Christ our Teacher and Lord— towards solving the problem of authority'

20 Mt. 4.10
21 Mk. 8.31
22 Mt. 26.54
23 Lk. 24.26, 44
24 Lk. 10.26
25 Mk. 12.10
26 Mk. 7.9, 13
27 Mk. 12.24
28 Jn. 10.35
29 Mt. 5.18
30 Lk. 6.12, 13
31 e.g. 2 Cor. 8.23; Acts 13.1–3; 14.14; Phil. 2.25
32 Acts 26.12.cf. 9.1, 2 and 22.5
33 Mt. 10.40; Jn. 13.20
34 Gal. 1.1
35 Acts 26.17 cf. 22.21
36 Mk. 3.14
37 Jn. 15.27
38 cf. 1 Jn. 1.1–3
39 Acts. 1.21–26
40 Gal. 1.11, 12, 17, 18
41 1 Cor. 9.1
42 1 Cor. 15.8, 9
43 Jn. 14.25, 26; 16.12, 13
44 cf. Acts 1.1, 2; 2.43; 5.12
45 2 Cor. 12.12
46 Heb. 2.3, 4
47 2 Thess. 3.4, 6, 10, 12, 14
48 2 Cor. 13.3
49 Gal. 4.14
50 e.g. 3 Jn. 9
51 1 Jn. 4.6
52 see Eusebius' *Ecclesiastical History* III.xxxix, 15 and Irenaeus' *Adversus Haereses* III.1.i
53 Phil. 2.7
54 Mk. 13.32
55 e.g. Jn. 7.14–17; 12.49; 17.8
56 Jn. 13.13

# Have you seen
# The Scripture Union
# KEY BOOKS
# Range?

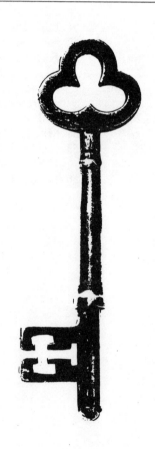

## UNDERSTANDING CHRISTIAN ATTITUDES
George Hoffman

The author deals positively and clearly with the Christian approach to a wide number of social and moral problems.

## UNDERSTANDING THE SUPERNATURAL
Canon Stafford Wright

A timely assessment of the occult based on the warnings given in the Bible and the Christian's understanding of the power of Christ and the nature of evil.

## UNDERSTANDING THE TEN COMMANDMENTS
John Eddison

The author considers the relevance of the Ten Commandments to contemporary life.

## UNDERSTANDING OURSELVES
John Eddison

A sympathetic, Christian view of the anxiety and depression that trouble so many in today's world.

## UNDERSTANDING THE WAY
Robinson and Winward

A practical guide to the Christian life.

## UNDERSTANDING CHRISTIAN ETHICS
Gilbert Kirby

The principal of the London Bible College considers the application of Christian teaching in dealing with contemporary problems from euthanasia to pornography.

## UNDERSTANDING BASIC BELIEFS
John Eddison

An outline of what Christians believe based on one of the great creeds of the Christian church.

## LET'S TALK IT THROUGH
J. Hills Cotterill

Discussion starters and background material on a variety of topics from contemporary portrayals of Jesus Christ to the use of music in worship. A mine of information.

## UNDERSTANDING LEADERSHIP
John Eddison

Ten studies on 'top men' of the Bible which aim to show exactly what the qualities are that make up a leader.

## UNDERSTANDING GOD'S PLAN
David Howard

A very readable commentary on the great themes of the book of Job and their message for us in today's world.

## UNDERSTANDING THE DEATH OF JESUS
John Eddison

A lively challenging look at the reasons why Jesus died on the cross and the implications of his death for us today.

## UNDERSTANDING THE CHRISTIAN AND SEX
M. O. Vincent

A trained psychiatrist explores the role of sex in the life of the world and of the individual Christian.

# DAILY BIBLE STUDY BOOKS

Thorough coverage of major Biblical passages combines scholarly insight with devotional warmth and practical experience. Studies of Biblical characters are also included.

**Man separated from God**  A. Skevington Wood
                             E. M. Blaiklock

**Jesus' Early Life**        H. L. Ellison
                             E. M. Blaiklock

**Jesus' True Identity**     James Philip
                             E. M. Blaiklock

**Man restored in Christ**   W. L. Lane
                             E. M. Blaiklock

**God the Holy Spirit**      Leon Morris
                             E. M. Blaiklock

**Christ Living with Him**   J. I. Packer
                             E. M. Blaiklock

**God's Kingdom and Church** F. F. Bruce
                             E. M. Blaiklock

**Christ the Way to God**    R. A. Finlayson
                             E. M. Blaiklock

# UNDERSTANDING THE NEW TESTAMENT

Based on Scripture Union's popular *Daily Bible Commentary* in four volumes these ten books offer a unique combination of daily Bible readings with the depth of a commentary.

**St Matthew**                   F. F. Bruce

**St Mark**                      I. H. Marshall

**St Luke**                      E. M. Blaiklock

**St John**                      R. E. Nixon

**Acts**                         R. P. Martin

**Romans**                       E. M. Blaiklock

**1 Corinthians—Galatians**      R. P.Martin

**Ephesians—2 Thessalonians**    W. L. Lane

**1 Timothy—James**              Leon Morris

**1 Peter—Revelation**           H. L. Ellison

## SCRIPTURE UNION BIBLE DICTIONARIES

### DICTIONARY OF BIBLE WORDS
John Eddison

John Eddison looks at a range of Bible words that are unfamiliar in everyday English and explains their original meaning and modern significance.

### DICTIONARY OF BIBLE TIMES
Herbert Sundemo

With the help of maps, charts and over 200 line drawings the author covers, in one handy volume, topics ranging from geography to religious customs.

### DICTIONARY OF BIBLE PEOPLE
J. Stafford Wright

Over 500 entries covering the major characters in the Bible. All the relevant facts of their lives are detailed and discussed in a lively, memorable style.

**Your Own Personal Notes**

53

**Your Own Personal Notes**

**Your Own Personal Notes**

**Your Own Personal Notes**